better together*

*This book is best read together, grownup and kid.

a kids book about™ cancer

by Dr. Kelsie Storm & Sarah Porter

a kids book about™

A Kids Book About books are exclusively available online on the A Kids Book About website.

To share your stories, ask questions, or inquire about bulk purchases (schools, libraries, and nonprofits), please use the following email address:

hello@akidsbookabout.com

www.akidsbookabout.com

ISBN: 978-1-951253-18-9

In honor of all the babies, kids, teens, and young adults we've cared for who are just fighting to be themselves.

For Roe and Jack.

For Brynn and Emme.

Intro

Kids ask many questions and are curious about everything... even big and scary things. Sometimes these things are hard for adults to talk about. We worry that by talking about them, we make them bigger or scarier. But here's the thing, our silence can be the scariest thing to a kid. When we feel big emotions about something, our instinct is to protect our children from feeling those emotions. Often we shy away from talking about them at all.

Cancer can be big and scary. We feel big emotions about cancer.

In this book, we breakdown cancer to simple, factual statements that aren't as scary as we imagine they might be. We help grownups and kids think and talk about cancer in a way that is honest and straight forward. Maybe you know or love someone with cancer. Maybe you are someone with cancer. This book is designed to help get the conversation started.

This is a book about...

cancer.

You might not know the word cancer.

Or, the word may scare you.

Don't worry...

We're going to tell you all about what cancer is...

And what it is not.

Because things are less scary when we understand them better.

So, what is cancer, you ask?

Well, it's really complicated and we have to start by explaining what a cell is...

A cell is
something
that is so small
you can't
even see it,
but cells
make up your
whole body.

Imagine cells as millions of teeny tiny LEGOs all put together to make a leg or a bone.

When cells are normal,

they make your body work the way it's supposed to.

But sometimes...

**cells can change
and go crazy.**

**They can look different,
and act different...**

and grow too much
and too fast...

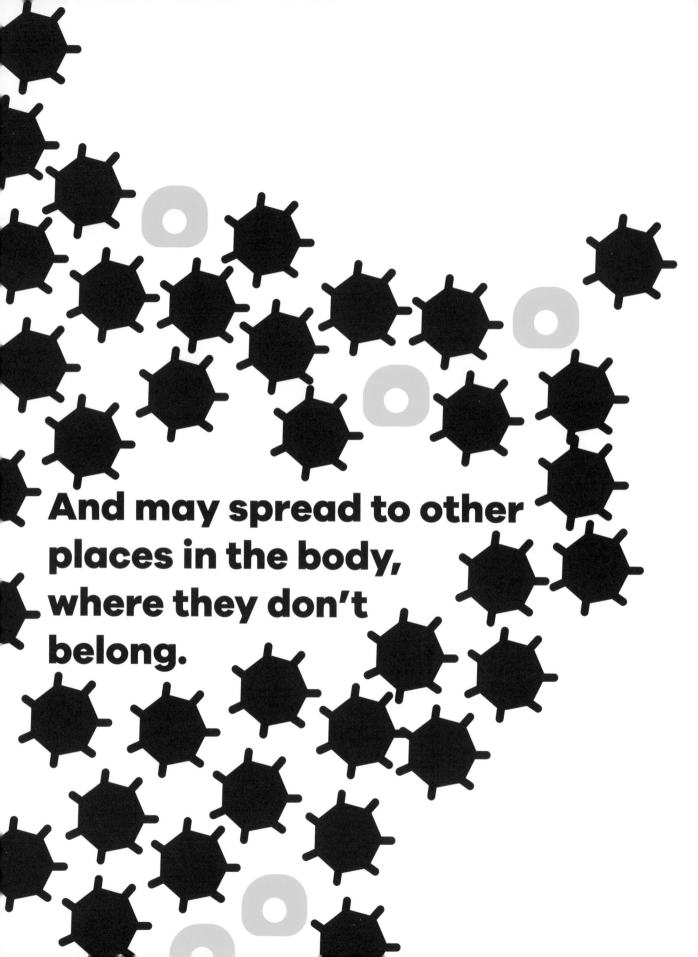

And may spread to other places in the body, where they don't belong.

Those crazy cells are called cancer.

When someone has those crazy cells in their body, we say...

They have cancer.

(Now that wasn't so complicated, was it?)

But there are a few things cancer is not.

Cancer's **not like when you have a cold.**

You can't get it from your friend or pass it to your brother.

Cancer is not
CONTA

GIOUS.

(That's a relief!)

And cancer doesn't happen...

because someone was bad or did something wrong.

It just happens.

So you might be thinking, who can get cancer?

The truth is...

Anyone.

Babies, kids, teens,
grownups, and
even really
really really old people.

But guess what? Most people don't get cancer.

REALLY,
most people don't!

But when someone does get cancer, it's serious.

Lots of kids wonder...

can someone die from cancer?

Yes...

some people do
die from cancer.

When you hear that,
it's OK if it sounds...

Sad, scary, no fun, unfair, or anything else you might be feeling.

Grownups have a hard time with it, too.

But guess what?

Most people who get cancer live and get better.

REALLY,

most people get better.

You might be wondering, How do people get better from cancer?

TREATMENT!

Treatment is a fancy word for things that make cancer go away.

Treatment can mean...

Surgery

which is an operation to cut the cancer out of the body.

Chemotherapy

which is super strong medicine that kills cancer cells.

Radiation

which is like an x-ray beam that shoots the cancer.

(Who knew there were so many different ways to kill cancer?!)

But treatment doesn't just happen in a day...

it can take weeks, months, or even years.

And dealing with cancer and treatment can be really hard...

YONE.

And it can cause a lot of feelings like...

loneliness, anger, sadness, anxi
fear, frustration, pain, fear, l
edom, joy, excitement, pride, be
ty, guilt, jealousy, rel
s, anger, sadne
ation, pai
ent,

Treatment can also be hard because people can feel and look sicker before they get better.

They may lose their hair.

(but it does grow back)

They might be extra tired.

They may not even want to eat.

They may look different.

Often when people look different...

People treat them differently.

That seems sad, no fun, and unfair, doesn't it?

Because cancer doesn't change who they are.

They still like the same things they did before...

You can touch them, hug them, or give them a high five.

You can watch a movie, make slime, or build LEGOs with them.

You can tell them about your day and ask about theirs.

You can treat them like they're normal, because they are.

That's how we all want to be treated.

That's it!

Now you know a whole bunch about what cancer is and what it's not.

You know how it gets treated and how you can treat people who have it.

And most of all, you know that cancer **doesn't change who people are.**

Outro

Now that you've made it to the end of the book, what comes next? Well, if you know or love someone with cancer, you may want to talk about how the facts in this book relate to the person you know or love.

What treatment are they getting? How do they seem different since getting cancer or starting treatment? Most importantly, how are they the same? What can you do to show love and acceptance to someone with cancer? How can you make the person with cancer feel normal?

How does what we talked about in this book apply to other people with disabilities or illnesses? How do we focus on who people are inside even when they look different on the outside?

We acknowledge the courage it took to read this book and hope the conversations it sparks are a little less scary.

find more kids books about

belonging, feminism, creativity, money, depression, failure, gratitude, adventure, racism, body image, and anxiety.

akidsbookabout.com

share your read*

*Tell somebody, post a photo, or give this book away to share what you care about.

@akidsbookabout